My Love Will Stay Forever

My sweet child,
have I ever told you that

there are more
than four seasons?

From a wonderful place,

comes the fifth season,
full of miracles and grace.

This fantastic season never goes away
or sends its glow astray.

This sweet season is my love
for you.

My love for you never changes.

It stays beautiful through the ages.

My love for you is
a special season,

full of joy
and reason.

With beautiful colors
like no others,

my love for you is always near
to help you thrive, my dear.

With amazing powers
like no others,

my love for you is always
here,

to help you grow
year after year.

My sweet child,

my love is yours,

all around the seasons,

now,

tomorrow,

and for always.

Day after day,

I promise,

my love will stay beautiful,
bold,
and kind
all the way.

My sweet child,
I love you,
and I will love you forever.

For my loving son,
there is only one season with you. - A.V.

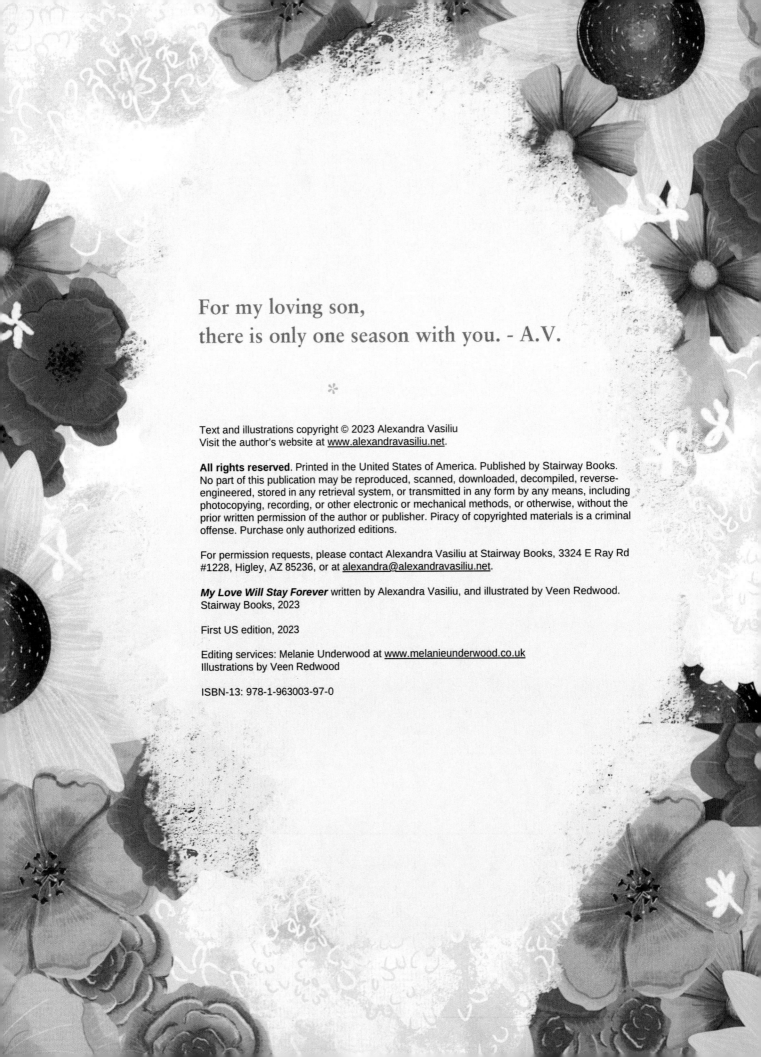

*

For permission requests, please contact Alexandra Vasiliu at Stairway Books, 3324 E Ray Rd #1228, Higley, AZ 85236, or at alexandra@alexandravasiliu.net.

My Love Will Stay Forever written by Alexandra Vasiliu, and illustrated by Veen Redwood.
Stairway Books, 2023

First US edition, 2023

Editing services: Melanie Underwood at www.melanieunderwood.co.uk
Illustrations by Veen Redwood

ISBN-13: 978-1-963003-97-0

Made in the USA
Las Vegas, NV
14 December 2023

82849731R00021